The Purposes of
THE LORD'S
SUPPER

PETER MASTERS

SWORD & TROWEL
METROPOLITAN TABERNACLE
LONDON

THE PURPOSES OF
THE LORD'S SUPPER

© Peter Masters 1995
This revised edition 2011

SWORD & TROWEL
Metropolitan Tabernacle
Elephant & Castle
London SE1 6SD

ISBN 978 1 899046 09 6

Cover design by Andrew Owen

Printed by Stephens & George, Merthyr Tydfil, UK

The Purposes of
the Lord's Supper

'For I have received of the Lord that which also I delivered unto you, That the Lord Jesus the same night in which he was betrayed took bread: and when he had given thanks, he brake it, and said, Take, eat: this is my body, which is broken for you: this do in remembrance of me' *(1 Corinthians 11.23-24).*

THESE BEAUTIFUL and familiar words, read so often at the Lord's Table, prepare us for a service designed by the Lord himself. The full passage (extending to the end of *1 Corinthians 11*) teaches the purposes of the Lord's Supper, and shows how spiritual benefit and blessing are to be derived from it.

Any study of the Lord's Supper must begin with the reminder that this ceremony is an *ordinance*, meaning that it was ordained by the Lord himself during his ministry on earth. The Saviour commanded his disciples – 'This do in remembrance of me,' and later repeated these words by direct revelation to Paul. There are only two symbolic ceremonies commanded by Christ for the New Testament age, these being baptism and the Lord's Supper. It is much better to call these *ordinances* than *sacraments*, as the latter is a pre-Reformation word which, strictly understood, means that blessing is channelled to people through the priestly use of symbols, so that the rituals themselves are powerful and grace-imparting.

Bible-Christians obviously deny that power or grace flows through a priest's cuffs, or through baptismal water or communion bread. The ordinances of baptism and the Lord's Supper are purely *symbolic* ceremonies, designed to remind God's people of great and foundational truths. The blessing does not come from the physical elements, but from personal appreciation of what these things represent. It is only as believers reflect on their *meaning*, praising God and pledging themselves to him, that their souls are strengthened, and he is glorified. Appreciation of the meaning is all-important. Without faith, the ordinances mean nothing and have no possible value.

In verse 26 of the passage in view, Paul makes this statement: 'For as often as ye eat this bread, and drink this cup, ye do shew the Lord's death till he come.' The Greek word translated *shew* means to proclaim or speak of something. The Lord's Table, therefore, is a message or sermon in symbols. It is a sermon prepared by the Lord, to which all his people are commanded to 'listen' on a regular basis.

It must be emphasised that the Lord's Supper *shows* something. It is not an efficacious activity but a teaching activity. The benefit is reaped in the hearts of those who receive a graphic reminder of great spiritual realities. Those who are moved by its message will repent of their sin, express their love to the Lord, and rededicate themselves to him. They will also rekindle their love to their fellow-believers.

We hardly need to add that the Lord's Supper is not a 'saving' ordinance. It is for those who are already believers. The Lord said, 'This do in remembrance of me.' If we have never known the Lord, how can we remember him? The Supper is strictly for those who discern the meaning *(1 Corinthians 11.29)*. The Lord's Supper does not *save*; it *reminds*, and its rich benefits come through the stirring up of mind and memory to appreciate once again what the Lord has done for us.

Before we consider the detailed benefits of the Lord's Supper, it is important to capture the general atmosphere, and to keep firmly in mind that there are two sides to its symbolism. It is, if you like, a *memorial*, in which we remember the terrible humiliation of the Lord and his dying agonies for us – a memorial of his *work* rather than his *Person*, for he is alive for evermore. There is, therefore, another side also. We must worship him as a risen Lord, knowing that his atoning death was wholly successful, enabling us to walk with him and love him. The memorial is held in the context of his being victorious, and we cannot shut this out of our minds. As we reflect on his death, stirring our sense of indebtedness and love, we nevertheless rejoice and glory in his triumph and reign.

If we come to the Lord's Supper omitting either of these aspects – the sorrow on the one hand, and the triumph on the other – we shall miss the point and the blessing also. Solemn reflection (including sorrow and repentance) must be combined with great gladness and thanksgiving in the correct approach to the Lord's Supper.

1. Safeguards sound doctrine in the church

A chief purpose of the Lord's Supper is clearly the preservation of sound doctrine throughout the churches of Christ. We are told that the Supper and its symbols must never be changed while time persists. ('Ye do shew the Lord's death *till he come*.') This Supper therefore reminds churches that they must never turn away from the doctrine of the atonement. Our theology must never change.

The great tragedy of Western lands is that in the historic Protestant denominations the overwhelming majority of ministers now take the opposite view from that just stated. They think that theology may and must change. Some years ago, when the principal of a key theological college denied the deity of Christ, he was vigorously defended by his church authorities. They insisted that he had both a right and a duty to advance his ideas, and to try to discover 'better ways' of understanding God.

The Lord's Supper rebukes that attitude, declaring that throughout the New Testament age – the last period of earth's history – Christ's broken body and poured out blood will be the dominating theme of the true faith, and the sole basis of salvation for sinners. Churches must never forget that Christ died as a scapegoat and sin-bearer for sinful men and women. Once this central doctrine is rejected, a church becomes 'no church', and even a 'synagogue of Satan'. The Lord's Supper exhibits and preserves the only ground of true salvation.

2. Moves individual believers to love

In the symbolism of the Lord's Supper every individual takes the bread and the wine, signifying that Christ's atoning work must be *personally* believed in and depended upon. We are saved as individuals. However, a believer's sense of grace may be quickly eroded away, leading to pride, coldness and backsliding. The Lord's Supper is provided to help believers retain and rekindle their humble indebtedness to the Lord. Are we frequently affected by Calvary? Are we moved to tears, as it were, when we think of what Christ went through for us to purchase us and make us his own? It is for this purpose that the Lord (who perfectly knows our needs) calls us to the Supper to spend a while focusing our minds upon his work for us.

What, exactly, are we to remember in the Lord's Supper? Is it enough to dwell on the death of Christ in a general way? Ideally, we must be more specific in order to reap the full benefit. For, when the Lord had given thanks and broken the bread, he said, 'Take, eat: this is *my body*.' We are to remember particularly his broken body. We are to remember that the Lord Jesus Christ assumed a real body, subject to hunger, tiredness and pain. This thought alone will kindle our amazement – that the Lord of Glory, the Prince of Life, out of love for us, humbled himself to the point of enduring all the limitations, pressures and pains of a weak and susceptible human body.

We should think of him as he moved towards Calvary, being punched, spat on and mocked, first by the scribes and elders, and then by the praetorian guard. We should think of him being stripped and scourged – a brutal, lacerating flogging reserved for slaves or those condemned to death. Then we should think of him having nails driven through his hands and feet, hanging in view of a sneering, hostile multitude.

Worst of all by far, we must think of him as he bared his soul to the searing agony of divine judgement, when that invisible, indescribable torrent of wrath and woe was poured out upon him, for our sakes. The pain of scourging, the nailing, and the open, bleeding wounds, were nothing by comparison with the intolerable, eternal weight of the punishment of our sin.

Truly – 'We may not know, we cannot tell, what pains he had to bear!' But we must try to grasp in some small measure the dying agonies, of body and soul, borne by the Lord – 'when sin with its crushing weight and killing curse, grounded, at last, upon that sinless soul.' A hymn by Henry Francis Lyte perfectly expresses our approach to the Lord's Supper:

> Dwell on the sight, my stony heart,
>   Till every pulse within
> Shall into contrite sorrow start,
>   And hate the thought of sin.
>
> Didst thou for me, my Saviour, brave
>   The scorn and scourge and gall,
> The nails, the thorns, the spear, the grave,
>   While I deserved them all?

A hymn by Isaac Watts expresses the same line of thought in an equally touching way:

> O, the sharp pangs of smarting pain
>   My dear Redeemer bore,
> When savage whips and rugged thorns
>   His sacred body tore.
>
> But my own sins, my cruel sins,
>   His chief tormentors were;
> For every sin became a nail,
>   And unbelief the spear.
>
> 'Twas I that brought such judgement down
>   Upon the guiltless One;
> Break, then, my heart, and weep my eyes!
>   To feel what I have done.

We remember that every moment of evil in our lives (if we are his children) was laid upon Christ. Every lie, every foul and loathsome deed, every evil word and thought, all our pride, indeed, every imaginable sin for which we deserved to die, was placed upon his holy soul. There, an entire eternity of punishment and wrath was somehow compressed into several hours of agony, that we might go free. Surely we must remember! How vividly Calvary is described in these verses adapted from Joseph Swain:

> *Such wrath as would kindle a hell*
> *Of never-abating despair*
> *For millions of sinners – then fell*
> *On Jesus, and spent itself there.*
>
> *'Twas justice that fell in that hour*
> *On Jesus our Saviour's dear head;*
> *Divinity's indwelling power*
> *Sustained him till nature was dead.*
>
> *No nearer we venture to gaze*
> *On sorrow so deep, so profound;*
> *But tread with amazement, and praise*
> *And reverence such hallowed ground.*

By causing us to reflect on Calvary, the Lord's Supper brings us to grieve afresh over our sin, and repent. It reignites our indebtedness, and causes us to commit ourselves once more to him. Above all it gives us a fresh realisation of the unfathomable, warm, personal love of Christ for each of his children, and of the great lengths to which he was prepared to go to express that love. We are moved to say in the words of Fergus Ferguson –

> *He lovèd me, and gave himself for me;*
> *And surely I myself to him will give;*
> *None, Jesus, will I ever love like thee,*
> *And to thy glory only will I live.*

3. Inspires gratitude and praise

The sorrows of the Supper are certainly intended to lead to gratitude and praise. To taste symbolically the body and blood of Christ is to remember that we have received the benefits of salvation, namely, new life, conversion, spiritual understanding, a new nature, spiritual and moral strength, comfort and consolation, and the certainty of everlasting glory. The symbolism of the Supper says, 'All these are yours, in Christ.'

We realise that the Supper was designed to encourage us by noting the circumstances in which it was first held. 'The Lord Jesus the *same night* in which he was betrayed took bread.' Before he went to Calvary, before the disciples were scattered, he prepared them for sorrows by giving them sight of the positive purpose to be served by his sufferings. 'I shall be taken,' he said, in effect, 'but this will not be the end of everything. This body will be broken, but it will be for you, and you will look back on this, and rejoice because of it.'

The Lord's Supper was inaugurated to communicate light and encouragement. When plunged into despair by events, the disciples would hopefully remember his words. And certainly they would later, as the Holy Spirit brought their full significance to their minds.

The record of that first Supper reads, 'And when he had given thanks, he brake it *[the bread]*.' Similarly, he gave thanks before pouring out the wine, for the record says – 'After the same manner also he took the cup.' Although the bread and wine symbolised his violent execution, the Lord nevertheless gave thanks for them. Thanksgiving, not sorrow, was the dominant theme of the first Supper; so it should be today. The Lord's Supper is meant to be an occasion when the soul rises and sings, glorying in the wonderful blessings of Christ.

The words, 'Take, eat,' as we have noted, speak of benefits. We have been invited to a supper, and it is an occasion for gladness. This moving, positive purpose of the Lord's Supper is captured in many hymns. Horatius Bonar writes:

> *This is the hour of banquet and of song;*
> *This is the heavenly table spread for me;*
> *Here let me feast, and feasting still prolong*
> *The brief, bright hour of fellowship with thee.*

Josiah Conder points to the same purpose of joy:

> *Here would I find a calm retreat,*
> *From vain distractions, near thy feet,*
> *And, borne above all earthly care,*
> *Be joyful in thy house of prayer.*

Isaac Watts focuses thankfulness on the amazing and unconditional favour of God in his grace:

> *While all our hearts and all our songs*
> *   Join to admire the feast,*
> *Each of us cry, with thankful tongue,*
> *   'Lord, why was I a guest?'*

Watts again emphasises gladness and joy in the following verses about the Lord's Supper:

> *Let every act of worship be*
> *Like our espousals, Lord, to thee;*
> *Like the dear hour when from above*
> *We first received thy pledge of love.*

> *The gladness of that happy day –*
> *Our hearts would wish it long to stay;*
> *Nor let our faith forsake its hold,*
> *Nor comfort sink, nor love grow cold.*

> *Each following minute as it flies,*
> *Increase thy praise, improve our joys,*
> *Till we are raised to sing thy name*
> *At the great Supper of the Lamb.*

4. Symbolises imputed righteousness

The broken bread and poured out wine distributed at the Lord's Supper also symbolise the imputed righteousness of Christ, which enables his people to draw near to the holy God, and to be pleasing to him. Look again at the words of Christ. He said, 'Take, eat: this is my body, which is broken for you.' The bread is not only broken to symbolise the blows of divine judgement, but also to picture the distribution of the benefits of Christ's atonement to his people.

The Son of God offered up his perfect righteousness on behalf of the redeemed, so that his perfections might purchase for them an eternal bliss. An atonement for sin was not, in a sense, enough. That, certainly, would deliver sinners from hell, but where would this leave them? Negatively, they would escape judgement, but positively, they would still have no right to Heaven. They would still have no merit, no worth, and no good works entitling them to an eternal reward. Christ also must earn their eternal blessedness, and his infinite righteousness has secured this. We remember at the Table, not only a dying, suffering Saviour, but One whose infinite righteousness in life was offered up, and 'distributed' to his people. We shelter under his blood, and also under his perfect offering of righteousness.

5. Reminds of privilege and security

A further positive theme symbolised in the Lord's Supper is that of the eternal covenant of grace. 'After the same manner also he took the cup, when he had supped, saying, This cup is the new testament in my blood: this do ye, as oft as ye drink it, in remembrance of me.' What is the 'new testament', or new covenant? The blood of Christ was shed in fulfilment of a covenant, or agreement, made between the members of the eternal Godhead in eternity past. This agreement may be summarised in the following imaginary conversation between Father and Son:–

The Father said to the Son, 'If you will go to earth to suffer, bleed and die on Calvary's cross to pay the price of sin, and to purchase and redeem the elect, I will give you that people for ever. I will bless them, and they shall be yours everlastingly.' Then the Son, for his part, said, 'I will gladly go and suffer and die for them, that they may be purchased, and brought safely home for all eternity.'

The blood of Christ is the purchase price of the new covenant. That price has been paid. The transaction has taken place, once and for ever. The infinitely just and faithful Father will never dishonour that greatest of all transactions, which can never fail or fall. The covenant is sure and certain.

Therefore, at the Lord's Supper we are able to reflect on the security that we have in Christ. When we take the wine (the symbol of that purchase price), it represents the highest price ever paid for anything. The entire universe and all history cannot equal the value of a single drop of the infinitely precious blood of Christ, the ransom price of God's children. At the Lord's Table the symbol of the blood of Christ is taken by each believer, signifying our individual guarantee of covenant safety in Christ. Christ's words are clear: 'I lay down my life for the sheep...And I give unto them eternal life; and they shall never perish, neither shall any man pluck them out of my hand.'

This blood, as we are told in *Hebrews*, is 'the blood of the everlasting covenant'. We are the privileged subjects of an eternal transaction. Our salvation is as safe and certain as the everlasting preciousness of the blood of Christ, ever revered by the Father. So the Lord's Table is a place of incomparable security; a place of comfort, and a place of favour. Here, we should give time to reflect on the absolute security of those who are the special objects of the love of Christ.

6. Emphasises the duty of holiness

The Lord's Table is a place of rededication in personal holiness. Mention of the covenant reminds us of this, for *Hebrews 10.16-17* says: 'This is the covenant that I will make with them after those days, saith the Lord, I will put my laws into their hearts, and in their minds will I write them; and their sins and iniquities will I remember no more.' The covenant purchased by the blood of Christ is a covenant of holiness! Righteousness is the Lord's purpose. The blood of the new covenant was shed not only for our forgiveness, but to purchase for us a new nature and a lively conscience, and to set us on the road of righteousness.

Have we remained conscientious in striving for improvement of character and conquering sin? Has this been our supreme concern? The Lord's Supper is a time for honest appraisal before God. In *1 Corinthians 11.27* Paul says: 'Wherefore whosoever shall eat this bread, and drink this cup of the Lord, unworthily, shall be guilty of the body and blood of the Lord.'

Earlier in the chapter the apostle had rebuked the Corinthians in these words: 'Now in this that I declare unto you I praise you not, that ye come together not for the better, but for the worse. For first of all, when ye come together in the church, I hear that there be divisions among you; and I partly believe it…When ye come together therefore into one place, this is not to eat the Lord's supper. For in eating every one taketh before other his own supper: and one is hungry, and another is drunken. What? have ye not houses to eat and to drink in?'

Some members of the church at Corinth had apparently slipped into great sin by their selfish disregard of others. These offenders had forgotten their calling to live as members of a godly family, and to show love and tenderness to one another. Linked to the Lord's Supper was a fellowship meal where the well-to-do disdained and disregarded the poor. Above all they had become indifferent to the price paid by Christ to purchase a *holy* people. Because of these things, their Supper became an offence to the Lord, and of no benefit to them, and they were severely rebuked.

Look again at the words – 'Wherefore whosoever shall eat this bread, and drink this cup of the Lord, unworthily, shall be guilty of the body and blood of the Lord.' If we come to the Lord's Table heedless, selfish, and indifferent to our fellowship obligations, we rank ourselves, in a sense, with those who crucified him. *They* were indifferent to his body. They did not value him or care what was happening to him, or what he was achieving. Insincerity at the Lord's Table ranks us with the crucifiers. Paul therefore gives the challenge – 'But let a man examine himself, and so let him eat of that bread, and drink of that cup. For he that eateth and drinketh unworthily, eateth and drinketh damnation to himself *[meaning here, judgement or discipline*], not discerning the Lord's body.'

---

* 'Damnation' in the *King James Version* is too strong a translation of the Greek 'judgement'.

In other words, the believer who comes insincerely and heedlessly to the Lord's Supper renders himself liable to chastisement from the Lord. It is no light matter to gather round the Lord's Table insincerely. Christ has ordained this symbolic service as an essential help and spur to our faith and to stir our obligation to holiness. To treat this with indifference is to incur displeasure and discipline. How careful we should be! Even before we come we ought to examine our hearts and repent of our sins – 'For if we would judge ourselves, we should not be judged' (verse 31).

To be insincere in this ordinance, and to have no respect for it as a 'regulator' of our behaviour, may even lead to the Lord sending sickness as a discipline, even fatal illness, as the apostle tells us in verse 30: 'For this cause many are weak and sickly among you, and many sleep.' Obviously, we must recognise that not all sickness is a discipline from the Lord, but on occasions it may be. It is a solemn thought that sickness may arise from insincerity at the Lord's Table.

The Lord's Supper is designed, among other things, to pull us up short, and make us consider our progress and conscientiousness in the pathway of holiness. It is a time for the renewing of our vows in this central objective of the life of faith.

7. Presents the Lord as our highest pleasure

There is another aspect of the broken bread, or Christ's distributed body, on which we should reflect, and this concerns our devotional life. If we are believers in Christ, *he* is our food. He is meant to be everything to us. There should be no greater source of encouragement, consolation, uplift and enjoyment to us than Christ, his Word, his purposes, his presence and his kingdom.

We should not say, 'I need this or that entertainment to have happiness and fulfilment. I must do or have this or that thing, or I cannot be satisfied.' We should say, 'Christ is all in all! He is everything to me.' The Lord's Supper reminds us of this. Christ, and the things of Christ constitute our best food and drink. At the Lord's Table we must take him, once again, to be our supreme source of satisfaction, happiness and peace, and we must repent if we have allowed anything to steal his place of pre-eminence in our lives and affections. We must surely pray in the spirit of Toplady's words:

> *Nothing, save Jesus, would I know;*
> *My friend and my companion thou!*
> *Lord, seize my heart, assert thy right,*
> *And put all other loves to flight.*
>
> *All idols—tread beneath thy feet,*
> *And to thyself the conquest get:*
> *Let sin no more oppose my Lord,*
> *Slain by the Spirit's two-edged sword.*

At the Lord's Table we shall long and pray for a greater view of the glorious Person of Christ, and a fuller interest in his purposes. Isaac Watts penned these exceptionally beautiful lines as his own prayer:

> *My Lord, my life, my love,*
> *To thee, to thee I call:*
> *I cannot live, if thou remove,*
> *For thou art All-in-all.*
>
> *The smilings of thy face,*
> *Such happiness they are!*
> *'Tis Heaven to rest in thine embrace,*
> *And nowhere else but there.*
>
> *Not all the earth or sky,*
> *Can one delight afford;*
> *No fleeting touch of deeper joy,*
> *Without thy presence, Lord.*
>
> *Thou art the source of love*
> *Whence all my pleasures flow;*
> *The sphere in which my interests move,*
> *And all my hopes below.*

There can be no higher pleasure, no greater wonder, and no deeper thought than that which he sends. The blessing of communion with Christ deserves special attention. We note that the picture of a spread table speaks of close fellowship and conversation. The Lord's Supper is not a formal or business lunch, but a family gathering, and it speaks particularly of friendship and affection. It portrays sons and daughters who have gathered to be glad in the presence of their King; to listen to him, admire him, enjoy his policies and plans, and to express their gratitude for his fatherly care of them.

The Lord's Supper is therefore a time to draw near. We shall enjoy his voice in the familiar and sublime passages of Scripture customarily read at the Table, and respond in hymns and prayers of gratitude. It will be a time, brief as it may be, to pour out our love in deep thoughts of our own, and to feel a sense, as we so often do, of his great love for us. The symbolism of the Lord's Table assures us that the Lord relates to us as children and friends. Here we may lay down our sorrows, sins and trials, and yield ourselves afresh to his sovereign, providential care, and his glorious service.

Christ alone is the Head of the Table. The minister who leads the service knows that he must be as unobtrusive as he can be. All who serve at the Table are merely servants. With the eye of faith, we desire to see this as the *Lord's* Table. It speaks of him; it points to him; it exalts him and it draws us to him. It reminds us that he will never leave us, nor forsake us.

8. Leads to union with one another

We may think of the special family feast in Bible times, when a father would draw his adult children around his table. He aimed to bring them together, not just physically, but in harmony and mutual supportiveness. Here is a view of the Lord's Supper. One of its purposes is to remind God's children that they are joined together in a family. It is possible for a Christian to love the Lord, and yet to live as an individual, standing aloof from the fellowship of God's people, perhaps even infected by ill-will, and caught up in unworthy feuds.

The Lord calls his people to come humbly *together* with a deep sense of kinship. A fresh realisation must dawn upon them that they are equally children of Christ, loved by him, and purchased by his sufferings. How can they cry out for fresh pardon from God, without forgiving each other?

The Table is furnished with guests, but who are these guests? At the first Lord's Supper they were the disciples, Christ's chosen companions and servants. The risen Lord still calls his servants to gather round him, and we cannot come to the Lord's Supper without seeing ourselves as members of a privileged circle – a team, a firm, a mission, a faculty, a family. The Lord gathers together his own, his loved ones, his redeemed ones, his trusted ones, his elected and appointed ones, his children and his messengers. At this privileged event, we pledge ourselves once again to him, and also to one another, to walk humbly, and to treat each other with gracious dignity and affection, just as the Lord deals with us.

> *How sweet, how heavenly is the sight*
> *When those who love their Lord,*
> *In one another's peace delight,*
> *And so fulfil his Word!*

9. Prepares us for rejection by the world

Another truth clearly illustrated by the Lord's Supper is the fact that the kingdom of God is subject to rejection and hostility until the end of the age. The Supper reminds us that a vindictive world heaped all malice and violent rage upon the King himself. What will it do to his followers? 'The servant is not greater than his lord,' said Christ. 'If they have persecuted me, they will also persecute you.'

We are reminded in the Supper to expect nothing wonderful from the world, so that we shall not be disappointed. We are here to save lost sinners out of the world, and to help them to escape from its bondage. As a 'system', it is a sinful world, and even when it smiles on the Lord's messengers, there is still latent resentment and opposition. The events of the Lord's humiliation and rejection cause us to keep the world in perspective, and never to invest our hopes in it, or depend upon it overmuch. If it hated him, it will hate us also.

We too must be ready to suffer. It may be that we shall meet with hostility from some in our family circle, or from work-colleagues. We may be persecuted both in great and small ways. Certainly we shall be scorned by many. The thought of a suffering Saviour reminds us that this present life is not the time of entire peace and happiness. This is the time of spiritual warfare and striving for the Lord.

The Lord's Supper reminds us we are members of a 'foreign' community, but because Christ is present, we may be sure that he will observe all our exertions and afflictions, will bless and sustain us, and one day mightily reward us.

A Plan for Reflection

'For I have received of the Lord that which also I delivered
unto you, That the Lord Jesus the same night in which he was betrayed
took bread: and when he had given thanks, he brake it, and said,
Take, eat: this is my body, which is broken for you:
this do in remembrance of me.

'After the same manner also he took the cup, when he had supped,
saying, This cup is the new testament in my blood: this do ye, as oft as ye
drink it, in remembrance of me. For as often as ye eat this bread, and
drink this cup, ye do shew the Lord's death till he come…

'But let a man examine himself, and so let him eat of that
bread, and drink of that cup…

'Wherefore, my brethren, when ye come together to eat, tarry
one for another' *(1 Corinthians 11.23-26, 28, 33)*.

Five helpful directions for thought at the Lord's Supper

WE MAY ASK – What should we mainly reflect on and pray about at the Lord's Table? The scope seems to be so wide; how can we best order our thoughts, and avoid confusion? The words of Paul in *1 Corinthians 11.23-33* have for generations been presented by preachers as a series of directions for thinking. Many sermons of past pulpit worthies (including Spurgeon) show this to be an old and natural use of the passage.

It is observed that Paul's words may be seen as pointing the believer's thoughts in up to five different 'directions', each suggesting a different avenue of reflection. This certainly provides an easy-to-remember summary of the chief purposes of the Lord's Supper. The idea is that we should first look *back*, then *up*, then *forward*, then *within*, and finally we must look *around* us. To read the *Corinthians* passage with these 'directions' in mind provides a memory-scaffold around each instruction. And if we should forget the directions, we need only read through the passage to be reminded of them, for they are so obvious.

Look back

The first verse of the passage (verse 23) provides the first heading or instruction for the Lord's Table – we are to *look back*. It reminds us of an historical event – the cross of Calvary. We may recapture in our hearts what it must have meant for the Lord Jesus to die in our place. With what degree of vividness are we to look back? The answer is given by the elements or symbols. The Lord says, 'This is my body, which is broken for you.'

We are to think especially about the physical and spiritual pain and humiliation suffered by the Saviour when he took our place. The broken bread, representing his body, indicates that we are not meant to approach the Supper in a theoretical manner, appreciating only at a mental level how the atoning death of Christ expiates our sin. We must identify with the anguish of the Lord as though we had seen it for ourselves.

The symbols teach us to think of how the Lord bore the storm of God's wrath, an avalanche of divine justice, in our place. We must be moved by these things so that we become filled with a fresh realisation of the great cost of our salvation, and of the amazing love of Christ for us.

Our reflection should include this realisation, that our Saviour *consciously* and *willingly* bore our debt. As he hung and suffered on

Calvary he could see in his mind's eye each one of the people for whom he died. Scripture teaches, 'When thou shalt make his soul an offering for sin, he shall see his seed' *(Isaiah 53.10)*. He, who knew his people from before the foundation of the world, certainly saw us as he suffered for our sin. As we think of these things we praise him and love him for all that he has done.

Look up

First, then, at the Lord's Table we *look back*. But then we must *look up*. Who died on Calvary? It was the Lord of Glory, the King of kings and Lord of lords. What is the difference between looking back and looking up? Having been moved afresh by what the Lord did for us when he was on earth, our thoughts must move on to reflect on his majesty, grace and power in Heaven. He is our royal representative in Heaven, our Great High Priest, seated at the right hand of the Father, making intercession for us.

As our thoughts move upward we will praise him for his infinite love, and his amazing kindness. He had no need to show such mercy and grace to us. Why should he have been so full of compassion to people who gave him no thought, except to slander him, and who would go on to give him so much trouble and disappointment even after their conversion? We will admire and worship him for his mighty attributes as God and King. We will also thank him for his constant care for us; his plans for us; his amazing patience; his all-surpassing wisdom; his programme of training, and his mighty power toward us.

Look forward

Then we are encouraged to look in another direction – *forward* – because the apostle says that at the Lord's Supper we 'shew the Lord's death till he come'. For a few moments at least, we must remind ourselves that the day is coming when we shall stand before him and see him as he is. It will be the moment we desire and long for. John

Cennick, an evangelist of the Great Awakening, expressed this in the following lines:

> *I long to touch the hand that once me blessed,*
> *Those feet that travelled to procure my rest,*
> *To see the wounded brow and that dear head*
> *That bowed, when on it all my sins were laid.*

There – at the end of this present era of time – we shall be among all Christ's people saved out of every age, and every land, and witness the vast and full fruit of all his pains. To look ahead presses us to renewed consecration. If we have been tempted to live too much for the vain things of this present life, or to be overwhelmed by passing worries, we shall realise afresh that all our love and energies should be devoted to the coming day of Christ. We shall give him our lives once again, promising to order our priorities so that he comes first in everything.

Look within

Then we must again change the direction of our thoughts, following the counsel of Paul, who said – 'Let a man examine himself, and so let him eat of that bread, and drink of that cup.' We must *look within*. One of the purposes of the Lord's Table, as we have seen, is to promote in us genuineness, humility and true repentance.

We must, then, look within, conscientiously examining our hearts, and renouncing our sins. True closeness to the Lord brings humbling, and a clear view of sin. Only by a sense of our unworthiness will we truly appreciate the Lord's mercy in wrapping around us his own garment of righteousness. If he did not cover up our imperfections we could not come to the Table at all, and we should always feel the truth of this.

Look around

Finally, the apostle's words urge us to *look around us*. 'Wherefore, my brethren, when ye come together to eat, tarry one for another.'

The holding of this Supper brings us round the same table. It is an ordinance which draws us together, emphasising that the Lord sets his people into local church families to prove the power of grace in harmonious relationships. We must 'look around' us and thank God for one another; for our spiritual family. The Lord uses this Supper to compel us to deal with unworthy divisions and offences between us. He lays a regular challenge across our path, an ordinance which should make us think about relationship matters which are wrong. We are prompted to sort out our affairs, and resolve causes of mutual offence. Then we may rejoice again that the Lord has placed us in our spiritual family to 'love one another'. In our thoughts we look around, and tell him we will gladly keep his commands.

* * *

It is often the case that we see Christ least when the pressures of life bear heavily on us, and trials oppress. It is then that a coldness sometimes spreads over the soul and we feel cut off from the Lord. Equally, grief or severe disappointment may steal our sense of God. These are the times when we most need the ordinance of remembering. At such times we need its restoring, enlivening help. Whether abounding or abased, full or hungry, whatever our spiritual or earthly state, Christ will strengthen us through the thoughtful participation in this ordinance. He has designed it for this very purpose. It is his special provision. He has commanded us to come, because it is his way of keeping us close to himself and to one another. What a privilege it is to be called to the Table of the Lord to proclaim his dying love, until he comes again!

Companion booklets by Dr Masters

Remember the Lord's Day
Why was the sabbath day instituted and does it continue now as the Lord's Day? If so, in what way has it changed with the coming of Christ? How should it be kept? This booklet responds to these and other questions, showing that the sabbath principle is still God's will for believers today.

Baptism, the Picture and its Purpose
This describes the fourfold pictorial message of baptism intended by God for the believer, the church, and the world. It also offers biblical reasons why baptism is for believers only, by immersion.

Stand for the Truth
This gives the biblical arguments for separation from false teaching, showing the positive value of this. Ten commonly-heard arguments in defence of 'inclusivism' (co-operation with Bible-denying groups in, for example, evangelism) are answered.

The Goal of Brotherly Love
The great goal is *philadelphia* love, a New Testament term indicating a depth and tenacity of love equal to the love of a blood tie. What obstructs and hinders this strong mutual affection among believers? Here is a searching treatment of a topic vital to the holiness and happiness of believers.

Your Reasonable Service in the Lord's Work
It is a sad fact that many Bible-believing Christians do not engage in any real service for the Lord. They loyally attend meetings for worship, and may give generous financial support, but they *do* very little. This booklet focuses on the strong terms of exhortation to Christian service found in the New Testament.

Tithing – The Privilege of Christian Stewardship
This booklet presents biblical principles under a series of helpful headings. All the main questions about stewardship are answered, as the author draws Christians into the full blessing of belonging to the Lord.

The Power of Prayer Meetings
Why does the Lord want believers to pray together? Is this a biblical duty, or is it optional? What form should the prayer meeting ideally take? Dr Masters answers such questions and shows that 'corporate' prayer was commanded by Christ and given a unique promise of effectiveness.

Booklets and books by Dr Masters may be obtained from:
Tabernacle Bookshop, Metropolitan Tabernacle, Elephant & Castle, London SE1 6SD
www.TabernacleBookshop.org

Free online sermons by Dr Masters are available at www.MetropolitanTabernacle.org